Berger Science Readers

SPLASH!

A Book About
Whales and
Dolphins

DI059385

For Max,

a great fan of Berger Science Readers

—M.B. and G.B.

Special thanks to Laurie Roulston
of the Denver Museum of Natural History
for her expertise

Photography credits:

Cover: Kim Heacox/Peter Arnold, Inc.; Back cover: Dynamic Graphics/Picture Quest; Pages: 3: Getty Images; 4: Mark Carwardine/Peter Arnold, Inc.; 5: Mark Carwardine/Peter Arnold, Inc.; 6-7: Lefevre/Peter Arnold, Inc.; 8:Auscape/J-M LaRoque/Peter Arnold, Inc.; 9: Kelvin Aitken/Peter Arnold, Inc.; 10: George D. Lepp/Photo Researchers; 11: John Hyde/Bruce Coleman Inc.; 12: Francios Gohier/Photo Researchers; 13: Art Wolfe/Photo Researchers; 14-15: Doug Perrine/Peter Arnold, Inc.; 16: Michael Jozon/Seapics.com; 17: Michael Nolan/Seapics.com ; 18 (top): Doug Perrine/ Seapics.com; 18 (bottom): Norbert Wu; 20: Fred Bruemmer/Peter Arnold, Inc; 21: Windland Rice/Bruce Coleman Inc.; 22: Doug Perrine/Peter Arnold, Inc.; 23: Horst Schafer/Peter Arnold, Inc.; 24: DiMaggio/Kalish/Peter Arnold, Inc.; 25: Mike Couffer/ Bruce Coleman Inc.; 26-27: Francios Gohier/Photo Researchers; 28: Doc White/Seapics.com; 29: Ingrid Visser/ Seapics.com; 31: Stuart Westmorland/Getty Images; 32-33: Francios Gohier/Photo Researchers; 34: Tom Brakefield/Seapics.com; 35: Oswaldo Vasquez/Seapics.com; 37: Marilyn Kazmers/Seapics.com; 39: Ingrid Visser/Seapics.com. Photo Research: Sarah Longacre

ISBN: 0-439-80185-0

12 11 10 9 8 7 6 5 4 3 2 1   6 7 8 9 10 11/0
Printed in the U.S.A.
First revised edition, February 2006

Berger Science Readers

SPLASH!

A Book About
Whales and
Dolphins

by Melvin & Gilda Berger

SCHOLASTIC INC.

New York Toronto London Auckland Sydney
Mexico City New Delhi Hong Kong Buenos Aires

Chapter One

As Big as Big Can Be

All whales are big. But the **blue whale** is the BIGGEST.

- It's as high as a two-story building!
- It's as long as three buses!
- It's as heavy as twenty-five elephants!

The blue whale is the biggest animal that ever lived. It is even bigger than *Tyrannosaurus rex*!

Dolphins belong to the same family as whales. But most dolphins are not as big as most whales.

Whales look like fish. But they're not fish. Whales are mammals, just like dogs and cats, cows and horses, and people like us.

Like other mammals, a baby whale is born alive. It is born in shallow water, tail first. It may weigh as much as 4,000 pounds at birth. A baby whale is called a calf.

At first the calf rolls in the water like a barrel. But the mother quickly turns it right side up. Other whales help her push it to the surface. The calf takes its first breath of air.

Whales can swim soon after they
are born. The newborn calf feeds
on milk from its mother's body. The
mother squirts rich, oily, yellow milk
into the baby's mouth.

The young calf feeds many times
a day. Every day, it guzzles up to 130
gallons of milk. And every day, it gains
as much as 200 pounds! After about
one year, the calf is ready to find its
own food.

A whale is warm-blooded. This means it stays warm, no matter how cold the water.

Two heavy layers cover the whale's body like a blanket. The top layer is the whale's skin. It can be more than one foot thick! Underneath is a layer of fat. It is called blubber. The blubber can be more than two feet thick in places!

A whale breathes air just as you do. But it does not have a nose like yours. Instead, a whale breathes through an opening called a blowhole.

The blowhole is on top of the whale's head. This lets the whale breathe while most of its body stays underwater.

When a whale dives, it holds its breath. One breath goes a long way. Some whales can hold their breath for up to two hours. Try holding your breath. One minute is tops!

Sooner or later, a whale must breathe. Up it swims to the surface. It breathes out the air in its lungs.

One day, you may see a whale breathe out. The air mixes with water. It makes a cloud called a blow.

Not all blows are alike. Some go straight up. They can reach as high as a three-story building. Others spread out in a spray. They look like a fountain.

You can see some blows for miles. You can hear them for hundreds of feet. But did you know this? If you're close, you can smell them. Most whales have very bad breath!

Deep ocean water is dark and murky. It is hard for whales to see very far. But sound travels very well through water. So whales depend more on hearing than on sight.

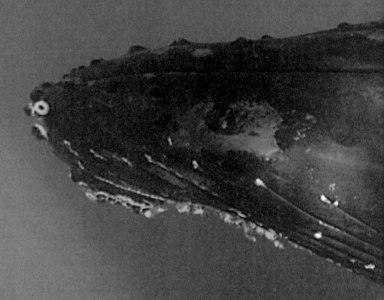

Whales have ears, but the ears are hard to spot. They are two tiny holes in the skin. Yet whales hear better than most people.

Whales can hear the different sounds that other whales make. They can hear one another miles apart. The sounds help keep them in touch.

Sounds help whales in another way. They let whales find objects underwater. The whale makes sounds. Then it listens for the echoes that bounce back.

Some echoes come back quickly. That means the object is close. Some echoes take longer to return. That means the object is far away. Using sounds to find things is called echolocation (ek-oh-loh-KAY-shun).

Chapter Two

Whales with Teeth

Most whales have teeth. They are called **toothed whales**. The teeth are for catching prey. They are not for chewing. Toothed whales swallow their food whole and alive.

The **sperm whale** is the biggest toothed whale. It's a huge animal in many ways. It has

- the biggest head of any whale,
- the largest brain,
- the thickest skin,
- and the heaviest layer of blubber.

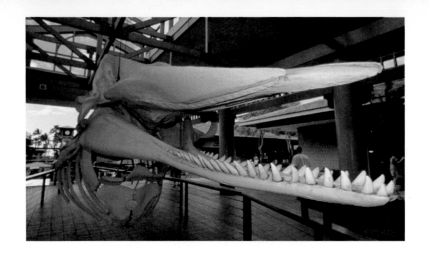

Fifty giant teeth line the sperm whale's lower jaw. Each tooth is several inches long. And each weighs half a pound.

The sperm whale eats many kinds of fish. But its favorite food looks like an octopus. It is called a **squid**. Instead of eight arms, a squid has ten arms.

Squid come in all sizes. Some are as small as cucumbers. Others are as big as canoes. The biggest ones are called **giant squid**.

Sperm whales hunt giant squid. The squid live at the bottom of the sea. Sperm whales dive very deep to catch them.

A sperm whale drops down, like a sleek submarine. After about a mile, it nears the ocean floor. It uses echolocation to find its prey.

A sperm whale can't always catch a giant squid. But when it does, the squid fights back. The whale and squid battle it out. But the whale usually wins. It swallows the huge squid.

Narwhals are much smaller than sperm whales. Most have only two teeth. In male narwhals, one tooth sticks straight out. It is eight feet long and comes to a sharp point. The tooth is called a tusk.

No one knows why male narwhals have tusks. They may be used to spear large fish, to dig shellfish out of the mud on the ocean bottom, or to attract females. The reason for the tusks is a mystery.

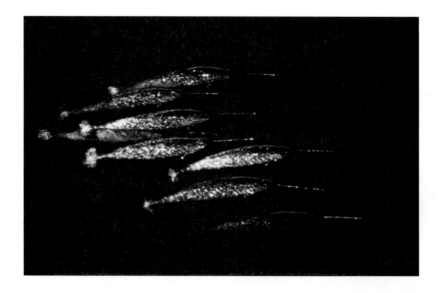

Chapter Three

Dolphins

Dolphins are small, toothed whales.
They are the biggest group of whales
with teeth.

Sailors tell stories about dolphins
saving people. Some years ago,
a woman fell out of her boat. Three
dolphins swam over. They held her
up in the water. And they slid her onto
a beach.

Dolphins help each other in much the same way. Let's say one dolphin in a group is sick or hurt. The others carry it through the water. They lift it to the surface to breathe. They protect it against enemies.

Dolphins are playful. They leap and turn in the water. The young rub up against each other. They play underwater tag.

People like to hear dolphins "talk." Each bark, squeal, squawk, or whistle seems to mean something different. Scientists listen carefully to these sounds. They try to discover the meanings.

You may know **bottle-nosed dolphins** the best. Often you see them in water parks and aquariums. Their beaks make them look like they are smiling and happy.

Bottlenoses seem to be very smart.
Trainers can teach them to play
basketball or to jump through hoops.
One bottlenose was the star of a TV show.

The **common dolphin** is smaller than the bottlenose. It's also a better swimmer.

Common dolphins often swim alongside big ships. The dolphins keep up with the ships, mile after mile. From time to time, the dolphins leap and flip in midair!

The biggest dolphin is the **orca**. It mainly feeds on fish and squid. But the orca also attacks other whales. It makes meals of penguins, seals, and walruses, too. Orcas have been known to eat birds and sea turtles. No wonder some people call the orca "killer whale."

Orcas hunt blue whales for their great big tongues! The tongue of a blue whale is an orca's favorite food.

Orcas live in all the world's oceans. Someday you may spot one. You'll see a six-foot-high fin sticking up from a male orca's back. It's a sight you'll never forget!

Chapter Four

Toothless Wonders

The largest whales have no teeth. Instead, hundreds of fuzzy plates hang down from their upper jaws. The plates are called baleen (buh-LEEN). They look and feel like giant fingernails. Baleen act as oversized strainers.

The blue whale is the largest baleen whale. As it swims, it opens its gigantic mouth very wide. Tons of water flow right in. The water holds millions of small, shrimplike creatures called krill.

The whale closes its mouth. Down comes the baleen. With its tongue, the whale squeezes the water out through the baleen. But the krill get stuck in the baleen plates. When the whale has enough krill, it swallows its dinner.

The blue whale has an amazing appetite. In one day, it gulps down about four tons of krill!

The **humpback whale** is another kind of baleen whale. You may think the humpback whale has a hump on its back. But it does not. The whale just humps — or shows its neck and back — when it dives!

Every now and then, the humpback flip-flops in the air. This is called breaching. The whale suddenly leaps out of the water. Its long, white flippers spread out like wings. Then the humpback falls into the water. *SPLASH!* The landing sounds like an exploding firecracker.

Humpback whales are the opera singers of the ocean. Their "songs" last up to 20 minutes. Each group of whales repeats its own song over and over again. They never seem to get tired of singing.

Right whales got their name long ago. Whalers said they were the "right" ones to hunt. They were slow swimmers and easy to catch. Also, their bodies held lots of blubber that the whalers wanted. People used the oil from blubber in lamps and for cooking.

Long ago, many right whales swam in the oceans. But hunters killed them in great numbers. Sad to say, few are left.

You can also tell a right whale
from far away. Its blow is divided.
From far away it looks like the letter V.
     Sometimes right whales are like
sailboats. Instead of sails, the whales
raise their tails in the air. The "sail-
tails"catch the wind. The wind pushes
the whales from deep to shallow water—
and back again.

Right whales sometimes beat the water with their tails. Or they jump from the water and crash back with a mighty splash. Sometimes one starts, then the others follow. Scientists wonder:

- Are the whales just being playful?
- Are they talking to each other?
- Or are they just following the leader?

Chapter Five

From Sea to Shining Sea

Whales live in all the oceans of the world. Most swim in groups called pods. Pods have from three to hundreds of whales.

Some whales spend part of the year in warm waters. In summer, they migrate, or move. They migrate to the cold waters near the North and South poles.

Day and night, the pod swims slowly through the water. The trip may take several months. The whales hardly stop to sleep or eat. In case of trouble, they help each other.

The whales stay in the cold waters for about three months. The waters have lots of food. Every day, the whales take in huge amounts of krill and other sea creatures. Their blubber gets very thick.

In time, the water begins to freeze. The whales migrate back to warm water. They hurry so they do not get trapped by the ice.

Finally, the whales reach the warm waters. Here the pregnant females give birth. The mother whale stays close to her calf. And she looks out for danger.

While in the warm waters, the whales stop eating. They live off the fat of their blubber.

Soon it is summer again. The whales gather in groups. They start their long journey back to the cold waters.

From time to time, a whale swims onto a beach. The whale is said to be stranded, or beached.

The stranded whale must find its way back into the sea. Out of the water, it is hard for whales to breathe.

Sometimes other whales hear the cries of a stranded whale. They come to its aid. Then they become stranded, too.

Stranded whales often live for several days. They may even get back into the water. Many times, people help. If not, the stranded whales die.

Once, a young whale was stranded. The U.S. Coast Guard found it. They named it Humphrey.

The sailors towed Humphrey into shallow water. Doctors examined the whale. They found many germs in its blowhole. So they gave the whale medicine.

In ten days, Humphrey was ready
to swim out to sea. Boats and
swimmers helped the whale swim
safely away.

One day you may find a stranded
whale. Call for help. While waiting,
keep away from the whale. Then maybe
your whale will live happily ever after—
just like Humphrey!

Index